Choose kindness

for Vivienne,
the kindest person I have known

ISBN: 9781073783908

'There is no need for temples; no need for complicated philosophy.
Our own brain, our own heart is our temple; the philosophy is kindness.'

~ HH the Dalai Lama

'The exalted state of enlightenment is nothing more than fully
knowing ourselves and our world, just as we are.'

~ Pema Chodron

From my heart to yours...

The purpose of this book is to share some thoughts on kindness and, in particular, self-kindness. Kindness is a choice and if we make a practice of choosing it, we will see our lives blossom. There's no doubt about that. Simply put: being kind makes for a happier life. I believe this is because it is our very nature to be kind, though sometimes we need to do a little work to remove the barriers that prevent us from seeing this.

The writing in this book comes from my own experiences and efforts in this area of personal development. The photographs were taken during mindful walks in the beautiful landscapes around my home. My hope is that the beauty of the images and the heartfelt words will resonate with others who are taking steps towards a more loving way of being. It's not always easy, but is a noble quest, because in loving yourself more and consequently those around you, you begin to change the world. I do not have all the answers – but I am sharing my thoughts 'from the road' in the hope that they may be of benefit.

I began to take self-care more seriously in 2015 when I came up close and personal to 'burn out'. Reactive fear, triggered by the 2011 Christchurch earthquakes, and then a series of family, career and personal traumas had consumed my reserves of energy and my body and mind were in a frazzled state of high anxiety and exhaustion. Thankfully, I realised where I was heading in time to be able to do something about it. But it was pretty drastic. I had to STOP!

It was a turning point. I realised that old patterns of behaviour that had dragged me through crises before were not going to work this time. I had reached empty and had to find another way. Burn out is a pretty horrible place to be – but it serves a purpose, it brings a message. It forces us to take a gentler approach to life. I realised that my 'iron will' and determination were actually contributing to the problem. I needed to be gentle with myself. *I needed to be kind.*

In addition to my mantra practice, which has always helped me to focus inward, I began a practice of heart-centred awareness. This simple sitting practice is rather like vipassana or insight meditation. It uses the breath to move into stillness and focuses on the heart as the centre of awareness. The heart is the seat of wisdom, and a direct connection to the love that is inside us all. The Chinese practice of Qigong recognises heart-centred awareness as a higher, metaphysical level of awareness. It is seen as a state of being that is beyond the normal fields of everyday consciousness. People call it presence or 'being in the moment'. It is tuning in to life *as it really is,* beyond the stories we tell ourselves, beyond the divisions we create. In meeting life as it really is, there is no numbing out or spiritual bypassing. It can feel quite raw and vulnerable. This is where we need courage. Pema Chodron calls it 'non-rejecting' in that we welcome all aspects of our lives and feelings, not favouring any in particular. It builds resilience and allows us to be of more benefit to others.

I am not a teacher. The words here stem from thoughts that have come to me as I've reflected on my own stumbling path. They come from many lessons learned (and still learning). I can claim no wisdom except that I do have what you have – my own good heart. And this is the greatest teacher of all.

Let this simple book be a place for gentle reflection; an inspiration and support; let it be a reminder – to choose kindness.

I choose to dwell in awareness.
I choose love as my foundation.
I choose kindness as my greatest power.

Let's declare peace on ourselves.
No more self-judgement; no more negative self-talk.

Sign a peace treaty with your soul:
"I promise to trust you and never speak harshly to you again."

Being present is a kindness you can give to yourself.
Don't dwell in painful past experiences.
Don't worry about the future – it will unfold just as it should.

Be thankful for this moment, right now. You are breathing; you are here.
The present moment will always be your sanctuary.

Be thankful for all that has led you to this very realisation.

The world is so beautiful but there is ugliness, too – violence and hatred are realities. But we can all do our bit to tip the balance. We can begin in our own lives by being kind to ourselves and those around us. This isn't always easy but it is the noblest path because...

... this is the way we change the world.

If, as the philosopher Alan Watts proclaimed, the Universe is experiencing itself through you – what will you teach it today?

Remember you are one of a kind. There has never been another soul like you, nor will there ever be. Allow yourself to shine as the beautiful being that you are.

Let yourself be found.

Rest in the beauty of this world; let it cradle you.
When you are broken-hearted, wrap yourself in a sunset.
Let the rain kiss your cheeks.

Know that the world belongs to you – and you belong to the world.

Rumi says "All that you seek is seeking you". So why struggle?
Just let go, and trust.

Enjoy what you have and more will follow.

Forgive today, because tomorrow you will need to be forgiven.

Some days all you can do is let go and love yourself in your brokenness. No fixing. Just acceptance. Just loving that wounded part anyway without judgement or hope of cure.

Love knows what to do – you just need to allow it.

Poor old Moon – constantly dragging the weight of the seas. Are you carrying some heavy emotions? The answer is always forgiveness. Forgive and let it go.

Forgive the other for letting you down. We all make mistakes. So be kind.

And if you are the one who messed up. *Forgive.* You can start again with fresh intention.

Are you paying attention!?

Sky sends messages in clouds: keep moving, keep changing...

...you are beautiful!

Let's not waste energy being strong and invincible
– instead, let's be soft and convincible.

Life is so much easier that way. Open up a crack. You never know, you might learn something. Just as fear can be cultivated through negative thoughts and stories, trust can be cultivated through positive thoughts and beliefs.

Trust is not gullible – it is confident and kind.
Trust says: 'No matter what happens, I can handle it.'

Sometimes we want people to be kind, but we don't realise that it is just not possible for them at that moment. We have to let go of expectations. If we contemplate the true meaning of compassion we realise that all of us are capable of being unkind. What is the remedy? Love.

Top up your own self-compassion first, because when you are full up with loving kindness it is easier to be kind to others, even when they are unkind to you.

When you are feeling down and unlovable, that's the time when you need to practice self-kindness the most. A quiet cup of tea, a pampering bath, some affirmations or words of encouragement.

Give yourself some love today – you don't have to earn it.

Everything feels a little better after a mindful walk in Nature.

Tell your troubles to the trees.

See how patient they are; how slow. Tune in to 'tree time' for a while. Ask them questions - you will hear the reply in your heart.

Take away the guilt and the 'shoulds' and what have you got? Is it possible, just for a day, to do as you please?

Put the 'to do' list away and replace it with one instruction:

enjoy!

Some days it's like sitting under a cloud. On those days be extra kind to yourself. It's ok to feel sad – let it be and know that soon enough the sun will come out. It is simply unrealistic to think you should be happy all the time. Welcome all feelings; they are part of being alive.

And being alive is the greatest gift of all.

When life gets really tough we want to escape!! We search desperately for a way out. But the way out is to stay with it. Non-rejecting. Pour some kindness on the hurt; meet yourself as you are right now. The hurt will pass.

You are a miracle – there is a space in your heart as big as the Universe. Your capacity for love is infinite.

We all experience the world through the lens of our own perception. So that means that there are as many realities as there are people. Does kindness feature in your reality?

What colour is your sky?

Resources

'Welcoming the Unwelcome' by Pema Chodron.
'Be Here Now' by Ram Dass
'Love for Imperfect Things' by Haemin Sunim
'Insights' by Barry Brailsford
'Life with my Guardian Angel' by Richard Bach
'Am I Being Kind' by Michael J Chase
'The Art of Happiness' by HH Dalai Lama and Howard C. Cutler
'A Gradual Awakening' by Stephen Levine
'The Miracle of Mindfulness' by Thich Nhat Hanh

Online

www.randomactsofkindness.org
www.theworldkindnessmovement.org
www.thinkkindness.org
www.bornthisway.foundation
www.channelkindness.org

Instagram sites with a mission of kindness

If you want more ideas and support about being kind, I recommend these Instagram accounts. They all have a message of kindness.

@kindnesscafes

@kindisbeautiful

@kindnessfactory

@thekindstrangerproject

@kindnessorg

@thekindnessrocksproject

@welivekindly

@channelkindness

@inserviceofothers

@foreverforwardtherapy

@kindness.source

@thekindnesscoach

@pink.lotus.yogi

@brittanykurp

@sarahfinds

@beautifulskybooks (that's me!!)

Kindness is a superpower! It destroys hatred and builds connection. Choose kindness.

About the author

Celia Coyne is a freelance writer and editor living in Christchurch, New Zealand. She has published non-fiction books and feature articles as well as short fiction. Find more of her writing and photographs at www.beautifulskybooks.com. You can also connect via Instagram @beautifulskybooks

Acknowledgements

If I really sat down and thought about it, there would be too many to thank individually. So I will just say thanks to my teachers and friends and even the strangers I meet who show me how to be kind. Special thanks to Richard Bach and the angels who said I really must get this book out there. Deep gratitude also to Ram Dass who passed recently. As he wisely said:'We are all in this together.'

Be kind, because it matters.

Printed in Great Britain
by Amazon

44793571R00028